The New Girl

Jennifer Degenhardt

To Lori, whose fabulous idea it was to offer this story in English for English language learners.

CONTENTS

ACKNOWLEDGEMENTS

Thank you to Gray Martin-Tsoupas for the beautiful cover art. It has been so much fun finding students to create covers for my books, and working with this artist is no exception.

Chapter 1
Cooper

My name is Cooper and I am 17 years old. I'm from Douglaston, Connecticut. I am tall, thin and athletic, too. I like soccer and hockey. I play sports for my high school.

The sports I like are soccer and hockey. I also like music, rock and pop. I don't like classical music. I also like to eat a lot. I like Italian and Chinese food. My favorite Italian restaurant is Rizzuto's and my favorite Chinese restaurant is Chang's. I like Italian and Chinese food a lot, but I don't like Japanese food.

I live with my family in Douglaston. In my family there are five people: my father, my mother, my sister, my brother and me. My father's name is Chip and he is 47 years old. My mother's name is Mitzi and she is 45 years old. My sister's name is Caitlin and she's 14 and my brother is Sam and he's 11. My family lives in a big house at 7 Settler's Trail. Our house is white. My family has three cars: my father has a car, my mother has a car and I have a car, too.

I am a student at Douglaston High School. My sister is a student there too. My brother is a student at Madison Middle School. My father works in a bank in New York City. My mother doesn't work, but she is a volunteer with many groups.

Chapter 2
Taruka

My name is Taruka[1] and I am 16 years old. I am originally from Bolivia, but now I live in Douglaston. I am new to Douglaston. I'm short. I am not fat, but I am not thin. I am in between. I like soccer a lot. My favorite team is the national team of Bolivia. I like…no, I love food! My family's favorite food is Bolivian food, of course! I like soup with noodles. I also like chicken, but the food I really love is a Bolivian food called *salteñas*[2].

---

[1] Taruka means "doe" in Quechua.
[2] Salteñas are a Bolivian baked empanada filled with pork, beef, chicken in a sweet and spicy sauce, and at times, peas and potatoes.

I live with my family in an apartment in a new development called "The Heights at Douglaston." In my family, there are six people. I live with my father, my mother, my sisters and my brother. My father's name is Pedro and my mother's name is Angela. My brother's name is

Oto. His real name is Otoronco[3]. It is a Quechua[4] name like mine. The name of one of my sisters is Inti[5] and my other sister's name is Wayna[6]. Oto is 19 years old and he works and studies at the local university. The name of the university is UCONN Strasberg. Inti is 12 years old and Wayna is 8. Inti goes to Madison Middle School and Wayna is a student at Pierson Elementary School.

My father works for a construction company called ME Construction. It's a company from Westchester, New York. My mother cleans houses for the families in Westmoreland. She works for a small, private company. My family lives in Douglaston now because the schools are really good.

---

[3] Otoronco means "mountain bear" in Quechua.
[4] Quechua is a group of indigenous peoples in the Central Andes and their languages.
[5] Inti means "sunshine" in Quechua.
[6] Wayna means "young" in Quechua.

Chapter 3
Cooper

School starts in two weeks. I need new school supplies. This year I have a lot of new classes: AP math, AP science, U.S. history, literature and Spanish 5. I don't have an art class because I don't like art. I like music, but I don't have a music class either.

I need to go to Staples. I'll take my Jeep to go buy the school supplies I need. I need notebooks, paper, pencils, pens and a new calculator. In my Jeep I listen to a song on the radio. The song is called *Stand by Me.*

Chapter 4
Taruka

It's nice weather for a summer morning.

"Mami, I'm going to work at the Greasy Spoon. Bye."

"Bye, Taruka."

I take the bus to my job. I'm a waitress at the Greasy Spoon. I work with other Hispanic people there. One man's name is Raúl and he is from Honduras. His brother Rafael works there too. One woman's name is Trinidad and she is Mexican. I like that I can speak Spanish with them. After work I will go to Staples because I need to buy some things for school. This year I will attend a new high school, Douglaston High School. I will have to take the bus because I don't have a car.

On the bus I listen to music on my iPhone. I listen to a new song by the singer, Prince Royce.

Prince Royce is of Dominican heritage from the Bronx and he sings in English and Spanish in the song *Stand by Me*.

Finally, at Staples I look for the school supplies I need for my classes. I will have new classes: biology, geometry, social studies, English, Spanish and chorus. And of course, I have P.E. or physical education. I'm not taking a computer class because I don't like technology much. So far, I have pens and pencils, but I need notebooks, folders and a new calculator.

At Staples, I find the folders and the calculator and now I will look for the notebooks. Suddenly, I see a handsome boy. He is thin and tall with blond hair and blue eyes. He is wearing a T-shirt that says, "Douglaston Soccer." How interesting. Maybe he's a student at Douglaston High School.

Chapter 5
Cooper

Grrrr… Where are the notebooks? I have the TI–89 calculator that I need for math with Mr. Coppock. AP math class is really hard, but it's interesting. Mr. Coppock is a good teacher. He is really nice too. I also found the paper, the pencils and the pens that I need. But I don't see the notebooks. I find the markers and the erasers, but not the notebooks.

Just then I see a very pretty girl. She is short, and has long, black, straight hair. She also has huge brown eyes. She is wearing a green shirt with the words "Greasy Spoon" on it. In her hand she has some new folders, pencils and notebooks.

"Hi," I say to her.

"Hi," she says.

"I need notebooks for school too. Do you know where they are?"

With a big smile she says, "They're in aisle 4."

"Great. Thank you," I say to her.

The girl doesn't say much, but she's very nice. And she's really pretty. I wonder if she goes to Douglaston High School?

Chapter 6
Cooper

I'm in the car on my way home. Tomorrow is the first day of soccer practice. I have some new shirts, new shorts, new socks and new sneakers.

"Hi, mom. Here's your credit card. I bought my school supplies. What's for dinner?"

"Your dad isn't coming home until 9PM. Your brother is at his friend's house, your sister is at ballet and I have a dinner with my friends. Here's twenty dollars to go get pizza.

"OK. Where's my soccer bag? I have practice tomorrow."

"Your bag is right here. You have everything you need for practice."

"Great. Thank you."

With my iPhone I write a text message to my friend, Kyle:

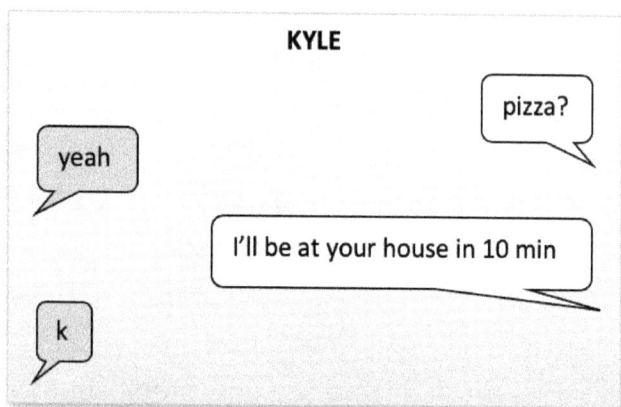

On the way to Kyle's house, I listen to the radio in my car. On the radio, I hear the song by Prince Royce, "Stand by Me." I like the song. And the lyrics are excellent. It's the song from the movie, "Stand by Me," but the words are in English and Spanish.

Kyle gets in the car. "Hi," he says.

"Hi," I say to him. "My family isn't home for dinner."

"My parents aren't home either. Typical."

"Yeah. But I don't like it. I like to eat dinner with my family."

"Yeah," Kyle responds. "We have practice tomorrow. Are you ready?"

"Yeah. And in two weeks school starts. I can't believe it!"

"But it's senior year. That's great!"

"True. True. Do you want to get ice cream after?"

"Good idea."

Chapter 7
Taruka

With the school supplies I bought, I take the bus to our new apartment in Douglaston. I ask myself: Who is that boy? He is very good-looking with his blond hair and blue eyes. Does he go to Douglaston High School? Does he play soccer? Will I see him again?

Arriving at the apartment, I say hello to my mom and little sisters. I need to organize my clothes for soccer tomorrow because it's the first day of practice. In my backpack, I have a shirt, shorts, socks sneakers, and a water bottle. I have to work after practice so I have my uniform in my backpack too.

"Taruuuuu," my mom yells to me. "I need your help in the kitchen."

"I'm coming."

I go to the kitchen and help my mom with dinner. I make a salad while my mom finishes cooking the chicken and rice. Right then, my dad arrives home from work.

"*Hola familia*!" he says. Then we all sit down to eat dinner.

Chapter 8
Taruka

I take my backpack and I walk to the high school which is only a few blocks from the apartment. When I arrive, I talk to the coach whose name is Coach White. I explain to her that I am new to Douglaston High School, but that I'm a good soccer player.

"Hi," she says to me. "What's your name?"

"My name is Taruka Fuentes," I respond.

"Welcome to Douglaston. First you need to warm up with the other girls on the team."

"Okay. Thank you."

I go with the group and we run on the track. On the field I see a familiar person. He is tall and handsome, and he has blond hair. Oh, it's the boy from the Staples. He must be a student here.

*****

Cooper

It's 10 o'clock in the morning. We practice for two hours and everyone is tired.

Kyle says to me, "Look at the new girl. She runs really fast."

"Yeah. She's really athletic. And really pretty too."

"What do you have to do this afternoon?" Kyle asks me.

"First, I have a session with my private trainer. And after I am going to play basketball at the Greenwidge Club. Do you want to play?"

"Yeah. Okay. Text me."
"Okay."

*****

Taruka

Soccer practice is great. I dribble the ball well and Coach White says, "Excellent, Taruka." After practice, I talk to one of the girls. Her name

17

is Emily. Emily is not tall or short and she has long, brown, curly hair.

"Is your name Taruka?" she asks me.

"Yes," I tell her.

"Hi. My name is Emily. And this is my friend, Caroline."

Caroline is very different from Emily. She is tall, very thin and has straight, blonde hair. Her hair is also really long.

"Hi, Caroline."

"Hi, Taruka. Your name is really interesting. I like it."

"Thank you. It's a Quechua name. My parents are from Bolivia," I explain to her.

"Really? That's great! Do you have brothers and sisters?" Caroline asks me.

"Three. An older brother and two younger sisters."

"My family has four kids too," says Caroline. "My brothers are twins and they're 15, and my younger sister is 8."

"Does your family speak Spanish?" asks Emily.

"Yes," I respond. "We speak Spanish at home, but I speak English with my brother and sisters too."

"Terrific," Emily and Caroline say.

"Well, girls. I need to go. I have to work."

"You work? Where?"

"I work at the Greasy Spoon. I'm a server."

"Ok. 'Bye."

"See you tomorrow at practice."

Chapter 9
Cooper

It's the first day of school. I go to all of my new classes and I see my friends. In the cafeteria during lunch we talk about the summer and sports. And of course, we talk about girls. Kyle isn't there so I send him a text:

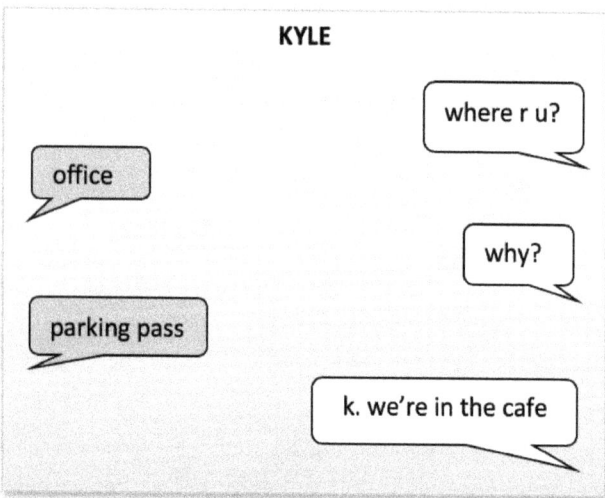

KYLE

where r u?

office

why?

parking pass

k. we're in the cafe

I talk to Matt, Ryan and Max. They all have been my friends since the 3rd grade. Kyle plays soccer with me, and Matt plays football. Ryan wrestles in the winter, and

Max… Max doesn't play sports. Max is the smart friend. He's the intellectual in the group.

"What classes do you have this year, Max?"

"I have AP math with Mr. Coppock, AP biology with Mr. T, U.S. history with Mr. Cabrera, literature with Ms. Ginn and Spanish 5 with that crazy teacher, Profe."

"Oooh. You have a lot of hard classes. Sorry."

"Those classes are easy for me. I am really smart."

"It's true. But you're not very smart with the girls!" I say to him.

"Ha ha!" Max says.

On the other side of the cafeteria I see the new girl.

"I'm going to talk to the new girl. Max, watch and learn. Ha, ha!"

*****

Taruka

I am in the cafeteria with my new friends from soccer, Emily and Caroline. Our soccer team is really good. We want to play in the state tournament.

Suddenly I see a boy. It's the boy from Staples, the boy who plays soccer for the high school.

"Hi," he says to me. "My name is Cooper."

I look at his blue eyes and I respond, "Hi. My name is Taruka."

"Nice to meet you."

"Same here."

"Are you new at school?"

"Yes."

"I saw you at Staples and with the soccer team."

"Oh, yes. In Staples!"

Emily and Caroline are really happy during the conversation.

"I like your name. It's really interesting," Cooper says.

"Thank you. It's a Quechua name."

"What's Quechua?" asks Cooper.

"Quechua is a group of indigenous people of Incan origin in Bolivia and Peru. It's also a language. For many indigenous people in Bolivia it is their first language."

"Fantastic! What's your last name?"

"I have two last names. Fuentes and Jiménez. Fuentes is my father's last name and Jiménez is my mother's last name."

"Why do you have two last names?"

"It's a Hispanic custom to have two last names. What's your full name?"

"My name is David Cooper Benenson, like my dad. But everyone calls me Cooper or Coop."

"Ohhhh, like my name… My name is Taruka but my friends call me Taru."

"Do you have Snapchat, Taru?"

"Of course. It's with my name, Taruka Fuentes.

"Is it okay if I send you a message?"

"Yes. I would like that."

"Well, I have class now."

"Me too. So happy to talk to you."

"Me too. Bye, Taruka."

"Bye, Cooper."

Caroline and Emily immediately start talking.

"How exciting, Taruka! Cooper Benenson is the best-looking and the most popular boy in the school! We're jealous! Ha, ha!"

*****

Cooper

"Coooooooooop!" Kyle says to me. "Who are you talking to?"

"Her name is Taruka. She's new at school. She's really nice. And she has pretty eyes."

24

"Ay, Coop. Every year it's a new girl for you."

"No, Kyle. This year is different."

"You say that every year. Let's go to class."

Chapter 10
Cooper

I send a message to Taruka on Snapchat.

Coop Benenson

Hi Taruka. It was nice talking to you today. Do you like Douglaston?

Taruka FJ

Hi! Yes, I do. Are there a lot of things to do here?

Coop Benenson

Of course. In the spring and fall my friends and I swim at Chelsea Port in Strasberg. In the summer we swim at Plant Beach. We also spend time playing sports.

Taruka FJ

I noticed. Many people play sports in Douglaston, right?

Coop Benenson

A LOT.

Taruka FJ

What do you do in the winter?

Coop Benenson

I play hockey with Kyle and Matt.

Taruka FJ

That's great!

Taruka FJ

Sorry Cooper but I need to take out the garbage and take care of my little sisters. We'll talk in school.

Coop Benenson

Ok. Bye.

Taruka FJ

Bye. See you later.

Chapter 11
Cooper

Tomorrow there's a dance at the Station. All of my friends are going: Ryan, Max, Kyle and Matt. I'm going too, but I want to go with Taruka. I invite her by sending her a text:

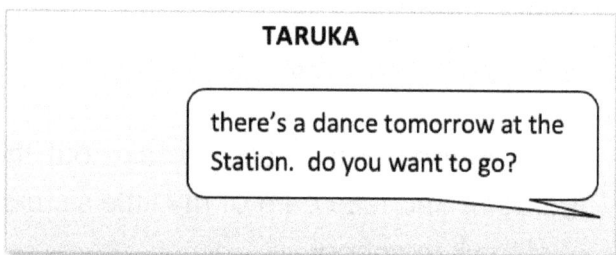

TARUKA

> there's a dance tomorrow at the Station. do you want to go?

*****

Taruka

I am in Mr. Coppock's math class. He is one of my favorite teachers. He is really funny and nice. I get a text on my phone. It's from Cooper. He wants to invite me to the dance tomorrow at the Station. I am responding to the text when Mr. Coppock says to me:

"Taruka, what are you doing?"

"Um, writing a text?"

"In math class?"

"Yes. It's really important," I say excitedly.

"Why is it important?" Mr. Coppock asks.

"A friend is inviting me to the dance tomorrow."

"Okay," Mr. Coppock says smiling.

With a smile I send a text to Cooper:

COOPER

there's a dance tomorrow at the Station. do you want to go?

what time?

at 8

yes, I'd like to go.

I'll be at your house at 7:30. pizza first?

"Okay, Taruka. Enough," says Mr. Coppock.

I don't have time to finish the conversation. I imagine a great night at the dance...

*****

Cooper

I don't get another text from Taruka. Does she want to go to get pizza with me? But in that moment, my phone vibrates. I have another text:

TARUKA

there's a dance tomorrow at the Station. do you want to go?

what time?

at 8

yes, I'd like to go.

I'll come by your house at 7:30. pizza first?

yes, I'd like to go and pizza is a good idea.

Chapter 12
Cooper

It's Friday night. I am wearing khaki pants and a new Vineyard Vines shirt. I like the shirt a lot, especially the color. It's purple.

Before leaving my house, I send a text to Taru:

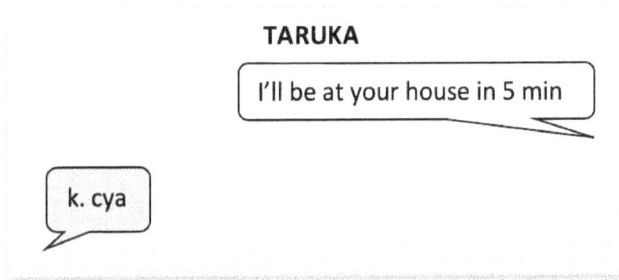

TARUKA

I'll be at your house in 5 min

k. cya

I go to Taruka's apartment. I knock on the door and I introduce myself to her mother.

"Hello, Ms. Fuentes. My name is Cooper. I am going out with Taruka tonight."

"It's a pleasure to meet you, Cooper.

One   moment," her   mom   says. "Taruuuuuuuuuuuu!"

"I'm coming, mom!"

Taruka comes to the door and talks with her mother for a moment.

"Bye, mom."
"Taru, you need to be home by 11."
"Okay. Thanks, mom."

Taruka gives her mom a kiss and she and I walk to my car.
"You have a good relationship with your mother, don't you?"
"Yes. She's really great."

*****

Taruka

After eating at the pizzeria, Cooper and I go to the Station. There are a lot of people there. Some boys and girls are dancing and others are talking with their friends. Cooper and I walk into the big room to find our friends. Kyle, Max and

Ryan are with Emily and Caroline. We talk about the dance and the music.

"How's the music?" I ask the girls.

"It's really good tonight. The DJ is Matt."

"Awesome," says Cooper. "I'm going to talk to him."

Cooper goes to talk to Matt. In a few minutes Matt plays a new song by Alicia Keys and Alejandro Sanz, *Looking for Paradise*. Cooper takes my hand and asks me to dance. What a great night!

Chapter 13
Cooper

Tonight Kyle, Max, Ryan, Matt and I watch a professional soccer game on TV. It's a game to qualify for the World Cup in Río de Janeiro. We are at Kyle's house when Kyle mentions the hockey banquet. Kyle, Matt and I play on the team.

"We need to steal that hockey sign for a gift for Coach G."

"Oh, yeah," says Ryan. "Let's go after the game."

*****

Taruka

All of the boys are at Kyle's house tonight to watch a soccer game. Emily, Caroline and I didn't want to go, so we are going shopping at the mall. I have money from my job and I want to buy a new dress to wear to school.

Emily and Caroline have their mothers' credit cards. They buy a lot more than I do, but I don't care.

In the mall, first we go to GAP. We see pants of all different colors: red, yellow, green, pink and light blue and of all sizes: small, medium and large. There are also orange shirts, yellow shirts, black shirts and white shirts. Caroline looks at the belts and takes two, a black one and a brown one

"How much is it?" asks Emily.

"$50."

"That's a good price," says Caroline.

Good price? For a belt? That's really expensive for me. But I don't say anything. I go to the section with the dresses. I see a white and blue dress that I like. It has a new, low price. The tag says that now the price is $23.95. That's a good price for a dress.

The girls and I pay and later we go to Abercrombie & Fitch. Abercrombie is next to the GAP. The music is really loud so we leave. We decide to go to H&M. I like H&M because the clothes are very colorful and the prices are good. We walk in the store. I see a skirt I like, but I don't like the color.

"I'm hungry," says Emily.

"Me, too," says Caroline.

"And I need some water. Let's go to the Food Court," says Emily.

The girls and I walk to the other side of the mall because the Food Court is far from H&M.

Chapter 14
Taruka

Cooper and I are friends now. We spend a lot of time together in school and on the weekends. I am not surprised when I receive a message from him on Snapchat one Friday:

Coop Benenson

Hi Taru. What are you doing tomorrow?

Boys don't write much in messages. I send him a message back:

Taruka FJ

Hi Cooper. I need to go to New York to visit my aunt. Do you want to go with me?

My aunt is my dad's younger sister. Her name is Ana and she's my favorite aunt. She is 35 years old and lives in East Harlem with her husband, José. He is Dominican-American. They have two kids, Sofía and Matías, who are my cousins. Sofía is 6 and Matías is 4. They have a lot of energy!

A message arrives on my phone:

Coop Benenson
Yes! I'd like to go with you.

East Harlem is a neighborhood of many immigrants. There are Puerto Ricans, Dominicans, Afro-Americans, Italians and Jewish people too. It's a very multicultural area.

Chapter 15
Cooper

On the day of the trip, Taruka and I take the Metro North train from the Douglaston station. We buy tickets and wait for the train on the platform.

In a few minutes, the train arrives and we get on. We talk for the 45 minutes it takes to get to New York.

"What are we going to do in New York, Taru?"

"Cooper, I have a great plan for the day. First, we are going to walk to a museum called Museo del Barrio to see all of the art by the famous Hispanic artists. The museum is open Wednesdays, Thursdays, Fridays and Saturdays. But it is closed on Sundays, Mondays and Tuesdays. After, we are going to look at the murals of other artists. The murals are on the buildings in the neighborhood.

"Interesting!" says Cooper.

Taruka and I hear the conductor say, "Harlem 125th Street" and we get off the train. We walk to the museum and we see a lot of murals. They are very colorful. I like them a lot. Many have images of typical life in the neighborhoods, but there are other murals too. We go to the museum and after, we walk to Taruka's aunt and uncle's apartment. While we are walking, Taruka describes the murals.

We need to bring a gift to the aunt and uncle, so we go into a small store. It has everything: fruit, vegetables, milk and flowers. We buy flowers for her aunt and some candies for the kids.

In Ana and José's apartment we talk a lot and the kids draw with markers. We eat *salteñas* that Ana prepares. The *salteñas* are so delicious.

On the train home, Taruka and I rest. We spent a great day in Spanish Harlem, a part of New York that is totally new to me.

Chapter 16
Taruka

It's the week of February vacation. I need to work three days this week. On Friday morning I'm at work when I see Cooper and his family come into the Greasy Spoon.

"Hi Cooper."

"Hi, Taru. This is my family. My mom Mitzi, my dad Chip, my sister Caitlin, and my brother Sam."

"Hi! Nice to meet you!"

"Hi. Can we see the menus?" asks Cooper's father.

"Um, yes…one minute."

I am surprised. Cooper's parents don't really talk to me. They don't even look at me. There's a problem and I don't like it.

The Benenson family eats breakfast and leaves. Cooper says to me:

"Bye, Taru. I'll text you later."

"Bye, Cooper."

*****

Cooper

After going to the Greasy Spoon, my mother and father have a conversation with me.

"Your friend is Hispanic," my mom says.

"Yes, Coop. You don't need problems," says my dad.

"Problems? Problems? Taruka is my girlfriend and it's not a problem," I say.

"Cooper, you are not of the same social class as she is. You need to go out with another kind of girl," says my mom.

"No! I like Taruka. She's my girlfriend!"

I have a lot of problems with my parents after that day. And I'm going to have many more. It's horrible.

Chapter 17
Taruka

"Taruuuuuuuu," my mom yells.

"Coming!"

I enter the kitchen where my mom is.

"Taruka Fuentes Jiménez, the boys in the newspaper, are they your friends?"

"What?" I ask my mom.

I read the article that explains that Kyle, Matt, Max and Cooper stole the hockey sign.

"Mom, it's not true. There's an explanation."

"Taruka, we didn't come to the United States to have problems. We are here for a better life."

"I know, mom. Cooper and his friends aren't bad. They're good."

"Taru, you can't see him anymore."

"But he's my boyfriend. He's my boyfriennnnnnnd."

That night I write a text to Cooper.

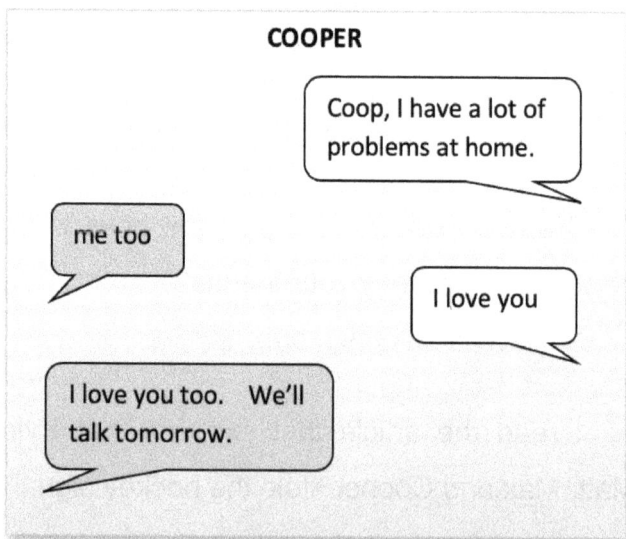

COOPER

> Coop, I have a lot of problems at home.

me too

> I love you

I love you too. We'll talk tomorrow.

Chapter 18
Cooper

Taruka and I need to talk. We have problems with our parents. I talk to her in the courtyard of the school:

"Taru, I want to be your boyfriend, but I have problems with my parents."

"Me too, Cooper. My mom says you're not a good kid."

"The situation is horrible. What do we do?"

"I have no idea."

*****

Taruka

After talking with Cooper, I go to visit my favorite teacher in her classroom. She is my teacher for Spanish 4 Honors.

"Seño, I have a big problem."

"What's going on, Taru?"

45

"Cooper is my boyfriend but my mom says he's not a good kid because of the problem with the sign. And his parents don't accept me because I'm Hispanic."

Seño Allen understands well. Her husband is Guatemalan. She says to me, "Taru, you need to talk to your parents. They need to understand the situation. Cooper is a good person. And you're a good person, too."

"Thank you, Seño."

When I'm in her classroom I hear a song. Seño loves music and always plays music in her classroom. It's a new song by Jason Mraz and Ximena Sariñana called *Suerte*.

*****

Cooper

Kyle and I are in the cafeteria. We have a free period because don't have a class. I talk with Kyle about the problems with Taruka. Kyle listens, but he doesn't say much. He

46

shows me a new song that has lyrics in English and Spanish. It's called *Suerte (Luck)*. Luck is what I need now.

I like the song. It's a song for Taruka and me... It gives me an idea. I'm going to talk to my parents tonight.

*****

At my house after dinner I talk to my parents about the comments that they made about Taruka.

"Mom. Dad. I want to talk to you about Taruka. She is my friend, but it's obvious that you have problems with her. Why?"

My dad speaks first:

"Coop. Your mother and I are worried about you. The people in this town talk a lot."
"Yes," my mom says. "The town doesn't like people who are different."
"But mom, dad, Taruka is a person. Yes, she's different, but she is a good person.

47

And, in my opinion we have to be nice to ALL people."

My father looks at me and speaks again:

"Cooper. You're a good kid and a good person. We are proud of you. You're right. People are people first. Differences don't matter."

My mom says, "Yes, Cooper. You are a good person. Thank you for teaching me. Do you have plans for the prom? You need to invite Taruka. Your father and I will have a party for your friends' parents that night."

"Oh, mom and dad, thank you! You're the best!"

Chapter 19
Cooper

It's a cold day in April. Normally April is cool and windy. But today it's cold and snowing. That's rare. Normally it snows in December, January, February and March. It doesn't snow in April. It's a gray day. I haven't talked to Taruka for a long time. But I want to talk to her. I want to invite her to the prom. I have an idea. I send a text to Kyle. He needs to help me.

I go to the football field. In the snow in huge letters I write "PROM?"

Taruka is in her art class. Kyle walks into the class to talk to her.

*****

Taruka

The day is awful. It's not sunny and it's not hot. It's snowing. I'm in my art class. I haven't talked to Cooper for a long time. Today I am really sad.

Just then, Kyle enters the class and takes me to the window. He says:

"Look."

In the snow in the middle of the field I see the word, "PROM?", and I see Cooper too. He has flowers in his hand. Immediately, I write him a text:

"Yes!"

Chapter 20
Taruka

Douglaston

Tuesday, April 15

Sign Stolen as a Gift

The students who took the sign Rer
Call

It's the end of May, the day of the prom. I
don't have problems anymore with my parents.
They read in the newspaper about the gift for the

coach. In a few minutes my parents and I are going to Cooper's house to take some photos before we take a bus to the prom. And while we are eating and dancing at the prom, all of the parents will have a party at the Benenson's. My mom made *salteñas* for the dinner.

We take a lot of photos at Cooper's house. After, all of my friends and I go to the W Hotel in Greenwidge. We have an excellent night. We eat a little and dance a lot. At the end of the night the DJ announces:

"This song is for Cooper and Taruka. It's a really special song. He plays the song, "Ella y él" by Ricardo Arjona, a popular singer from Guatemala.

Cooper and I dance the whole night. Life is good. Very good.

ABOUT THE AUTHOR

Jennifer Degenhardt taught high school Spanish for over 20 years. She realized her own students, many of whom had learning challenges, acquired language best through stories, so she began to write ones that she thought would appeal to them. She has been writing ever since.

Please check out the other titles by Jen Degenhardt available on Amazon:

La chica nueva | La Nouvelle Fille |The New Girl
La chica nueva (the ancillary/workbook
volume, Kindle book, audiobook)
El jersey|The Jersey |*Le Maillot*
Quince
La mochila | The Backpack
El viaje difícil|*Un Voyage Difficile*
La niñera
La última prueba
Los tres amigos | Three Friends | *Drei Freunde*
María María: un cuento de un huracán | María María:
A Story of a Storm | Maria Maria: un histoire d'un
orage
Debido a la tormenta
La lucha de la vida
Secretos

Follow Jen Degenhardt on Facebook, Instagram @jendegenhardt9, and Twitter @JenniferDegenh1 or visit the website, www.puenteslanguage.com to sign up to receive information on new releases and other events.

55

* 9 7 8 0 9 9 9 3 4 7 9 2 8 *